PREFACE

This book was written out of a heart to see lovers of Jesus grow closer to the Father. My desire is to see His children running free throughout the whole Earth loving Him and advancing His Kingdom. One of the most exciting scriptures, to me, is:

For to us a child is born,
to us a son is given;
and the government shall be upon his shoulder,
and his name shall be called
Wonderful Counselor, Mighty God,
Everlasting Father, Prince of Peace.
Of the increase of his government and of peace
there will be no end,
on the throne of David and over his kingdom,
to establish it and to uphold it
with justice and with righteousness
from this time forth and forevermore.
The zeal of the Lord of hosts will do this.
Isaiah 9:6-7

It is thrilling to know that the Kingdom of God will

continually advance, never shrink back, and that we get to be a part of the advancement!

One night as I was laying in bed in pain, frustrated that physical pain had continued for months on end keeping me from participating in activities with my family, I cried out to God asking Him why I was dealing with this torment.

He simply said, "My Kingdom is at hand."

I won't pretend that this made me feel better. I am fairly certain that my response had some attitude with it when I responded with, "but what do I do about it?"

He said, "My Kingdom is at hand, you only have to reach out and grab it."

At that moment I knew He was inviting me to find out how close His Kingdom is. I reached out into the air in front of me, grabbed a handful of air, and placed my hand on the area of pain. Instantly, the pain subsided!

We live in a Kingdom at hand: here, now, and within reach. It is my hope that as you read these pages you find healing and peace as you step further into the Kingdom of God, and it manifests in your life more and more everyday. I pray your faith increases so much that when you don't know what to do, you reach out in faith not sight, grab hold of the Kingdom, and place it on your situation.

I wrote this book primarily with those looking for the "more" in mind. Maybe you have all the answers or maybe someone turned you away when you tried to ask. This book is just a starting point in the journey of realizing what God has placed on the table for us, His children. Each topic contained in this book would require more than it's own book to go into depth on, and it hardly touches on all that the Kingdom has to offer. However, I wanted to create a launchpad for others to begin their journey from, and I trust that the more you seek, the more you will find.

Blessings in the discovery,
Cherish Bickel

CHERISH BICKEL

1

TABLE OF CONTENTS

CHAPTER 1

The Kingdom

So in Christ Jesus you are all children
of God through faith, for all of you who
were baptized into Christ have clothed
yourselves with Christ.
Galatians 3:26-27 NIV

When I was a little girl, I fell in love with Jesus. I knew Him and loved Him-He was my best friend! I recall well how after asking to be baptized, the pastor had counseling sessions with me to be sure I understood what I was doing. I can remember a feeling of devastation at the thought of not being allowed to be baptized because I loved Jesus so deeply and had already given Him my whole life. I didn't know Him to be angry, cruel, or strict.

However, as time passed, I was told that God the Father was distant, stoic, unemotional, and had a mean streak of judgment. I even recall being told not to read the Old Testament first because "God was mean back then." This left me confused as I knew Jesus to be kind, gentle, loving, and patient as well as the fact He perfectly reveals the Father. To further add to the confusion, my earthly father left a stain on what fatherhood looked like. For years, while knowing Jesus, I shied away from having a relationship with God, and to be honest, I didn't even understand how it was possible.

There were so many inconsistencies with what I was being taught. God couldn't be around a sinner such as myself? But if God fills the fullness of the Heavens and the Earth, He cannot be away from sin, He is inescapable, He is the God who is known for showing up in the darkest of places where His light will be noticed the most.

Furthermore, Christ, who is a part of the triune Godhead, bore our sin and shame on the cross and then went to the grave to preach to the imprisoned spirits who were made up disobedient sinful people. Let me not fail to mention that God in the flesh walked among humanity for over 30 years and ate with the most sinful outcasts of the day.

> For Christ also suffered once for sins, the righteous for the unrighteous, to bring you to God. He was put to death in the body but made alive in the Spirit. After being made

alive, he went and made proclamation
to the imprisoned spirits to those who
were disobedient long ago when God
waited patiently in the days of Noah.

1 Peter 3:18-20 NIV

In addition, we also have been made holy, blameless,
and a royal priesthood, therefore we are no longer
sinners, Christ died to take away that title. An angry
God sent a loving son to save us? Or in love were we
predestined for adoption which was all a part of His
good pleasure?

Praise be to the God and Father of our
Lord Jesus Christ, who has blessed us in
the heavenly realms with every spiritual
blessing in Christ. For he chose us in him
before the creation of the world to be
holy and blameless in his sight. In love,
he predestined us for adoption to sonship
through Jesus Christ, in accordance with
his pleasure and will— to the praise of
his glorious grace, which he has freely
given us in the One he loves. In Him we
have redemption through his blood, the
forgiveness of sins, in accordance with the
riches of God's grace that he lavished on
us. With all wisdom and understanding,
he made known to us the mystery of

his will according to his good pleasure,
which he purposed in Christ, to be put
into effect when the times reach their
fulfillment—to bring unity to all things
in heaven and on earth under Christ.

Ephesians 1:3-10 NIV

God lovingly and patiently waited and allowed me to learn the truth about His character and goodness, and I joyfully walked into a relationship directly with Him. I was now free to boldly and confidently go before His throne, unhindered by the lies of the world about His true nature. Until that moment, I was living in the Kingdom, but not in the palace. Allow me to share a piece of the story that God began to reveal to me to show some of the workings of His Kingdom and my place is in it.

Once upon a time, there was a beautiful Kingdom filled with wonderful people. The Kingdom was filled with light, color, and beauty. In this Kingdom was a young orphan girl. Though she was an orphan she always had what she needed. Her best friend was a baker who always supplied bread to the girl. She would visit the baker frequently, confide in the baker, and learn from him. He spoke wisdom into her life and brought peace and joy to her life. She never went hungry, in fact, she always left with her arms fully loaded with bread.

The King would walk around the marketplace and take note of the Kingdom. He kept His eye on this young orphan girl and made sure she received what she needed. One day, the King came to the young orphan and offered to adopt her. She was unsure what adoption meant and she was fearful as she had always heard that the King was a hard master with many rules. She would rather live alone than be a slave to someone. She told Him no and went on about her way still in the Kingdom, serving the King but afraid to get too close to Him. The King continued to watch over her and continued to supply her needs without her realizing it-often leaving gifts for her to find.

At last, while talking to the baker about the King, the baker told the girl she should give the King a chance and that He may be better than what others had said. Shortly after that the King came to the orphan again and offered her a place as His daughter. Though timid, she accepted and followed Him to the castle.

He showed her a beautiful room already prepared for her, complete with a beautiful princess gown designed just for her.

He asked her to get dressed and come to dinner. Still unsure as to all the unfamiliarity the castle and gown held, she dressed and came to the large dining room. The King greeted her at the door, walked her in, and told her that she was free to feast any time she wanted. The food would always be available and never run out. The heavy wooden table seemed to stretch on forever, and she had never seen such a variety of food before. She didn't know where to start. It was at this moment that she also began to realize how many children were there. They seemed to be everywhere, and they were all joyfully feasting as they moved about, coming and going as they pleased. Some sat and feasted beyond being stuffed while others grabbed a bite and ran off to play.

Over time the girl began to realize how truly kind and loving the King really was and began to see Him as a Father. However, she still felt out of place among others and was still trying to sort out what adoption meant. She would often put her old orphan clothes back on and hide. The girl was more comfortable as an orphan since she had no understanding of what it meant to be a daughter. At times she would sneak in and pick crumbs up off the floor rather than feasting on the never-ending supply of good foods. It was what she had always known.

One day, another young girl, a daughter, caught her hiding in her orphan clothes nibbling on crumbs. She told her that all the children there had also been adopted from orphanhood and that she had a place among them as an equal. The girl explained that adoption by the King meant that you were given authority in the kingdom and you were no longer an orphan, alone to scavenge for herself. She explained that they had access to everything that was the Kings. She had not realized that these children were once orphans from outside of the castle as well and that she was not an outsider among them. Over time she put on the orphan clothes less and less, choosing instead the clothes made especially for her and prepared for her even before she entered the castle. She began to learn her identity as a daughter and coheir as she spent more time with the King, her Father.

As time went on, her Father began to reveal to her the times He was in the marketplace with her, loving her, caring for her, and protecting her. His love was there all along calling her into a relationship with Him.

In the following chapters, we will discuss many of the elements of this story and the further revelation that God has shown me as I have walked closer with Him in the castle.

CHERISH BICKEL

CHAPTER 2

In His Presence

Therefore, since we have a great high priest
who has ascended into heaven, Jesus the
Son of God, let us hold firmly to the faith
we profess. For we do not have a high
priest who is unable to empathize with our
weaknesses, but we have one who has been
tempted in every way, just as we are—yet
he did not sin. Let us then approach God's
throne of grace with confidence, so that we
may receive mercy and find grace to help us
in our time of need.
Hebrews 4:14-16 NIV

The marketplace of the Kingdom was a wonderful place. It was filled with joy and goodness, even though it was filled with many orphans who were trying their best to find the truth. Everyone loved one another and served their King with delight! There was great respect for the King to the point of keeping at a distance.

This is where many Christians live their life. They love God and would give their life in service to Him, but they have yet to step into adoption, living with God as their Father and not just as a servant in His Kingdom. This might be rubbing you wrong about now, and that is okay. I remember a time when I would vigorously defend my position as only a servant of God. The problem lies in seeing this issue in black and white, one way or the other. We are children of God who give ourselves as bondservants-willfully serving from adoration, not forced labor. You can be both a loved child and a bondservant of the King. Your service comes from love and not from a striving or works-based mentality. There is a respect for the majesty of God, the greatness of who He is, that allows a holy fear and trembling, but it is vastly different from a fear of God who may smite you if you have a bad thought. The first fear is reverence, the second is better described as anxiety.

Many people are willing to accept Jesus and believe in God but are afraid of stepping into a relationship with Father God and coming to know Him personally. Either they have heard that He is fierce and stern, have difficulty identifying with a kind Father, or they have never thought about it. This can create a life of unwillingness to do anything unless they know for certain it is God's will. God is seen as distant and angry if you step out of line. This belief has a root in Greek thought that saw Heaven as a distant place, as well as misunderstanding of the God who was judge over the Old Testament, but Jesus declared that the Kingdom of Heaven was at hand, here reachable, and in our midst. The Old Testament needs to be read with an understanding of covenants and with the view of a Father who wants to protect His people.

God has a will and a great plan for our lives, but He does not desire robots as children. He has given us freedom and even gives us the desires of *our* hearts. He gave us imagination, giftings, and desires for a reason.

The fear of not acting in God's will can forever cripple you and prevent you from growing in your relationship with Father God. If my children were afraid of what I would say or do to the point they could not make decisions or trembled at the thought of doing something wrong, they would not grow in their relationship with me. Instead, they would pull away from me afraid that I might tear down whatever they had just built up, or worse yet, they would hide from me.

When we come to know the Father and delight ourselves in the Lord, our thoughts line up with His thoughts and our will shifts towards His will. Our lives begin to bear the fruit of the goodness of a life surrendered in love to Him. His desire is that all should come to know Him, if what you are doing lines up with that then you are surely living in His will until He calls you into a specific area. Even if we go in the wrong direction or miss what He is saying, He will lovingly guide us back.

Trust in the Lord and do good; dwell
in the land and enjoy safe pasture.
Take delight in the Lord, and he will
give you the desires of your heart.

Psalm 37:3-4 NIV

Come to know God the Father, delight in your relationship with Him, and allow His perfect love to cast out all fear, especially the fear of not pleasing Him and the fear of failure. His perfect love will cast out fear and erase the fear of punishment. As the fear of punishment dissipates, any remaining fear of being in His presence will as well. Again, this idea may not even seem like a "fear" in your mind, it may be buried so deep in your conscience that it seems laughable at first. It may be apparent as an idea or picture of what God looks like or what the throne room looks like. I'd say Heaven, but often people picture a bright happy warm Heaven, but a stone-cold God on a fierce-looking throne. A god who is ready to cast them out into the cold if they screw up. Allow Him to show you the truth.

Let go of the idea of being a perfect child, sober and unemotional, in His presence. He created you uniquely you. This is the same God who created the platypus, otters, playful kittens, and wild exuberant toddlers. He certainly has a sense of humor, amusement, and a love of individual traits.

Dance in His presence, paint in His presence, laugh and play in His presence, or pour out your heart wailing before Him. He is El Shaddai, God Almighty. He can handle every emotion you throw His way. Letting go of the fear of not pleasing God or not being good enough to be in His presence is one of the most transformative things a believer can do.

Release to Him every thought you have had about Him, every fear, and even every frustration. He wants to hear from you. He desires intimacy with you, an intimacy that is formed when we openly bear our heart to Him. Allow that pain to surface as you hand it to Him and wait for His response. He loves you through and through and is not ashamed of your questions, thoughts, or emotions.

As you let go in His presence, ask Him to reveal more to you. Often in these moments He pours identity into us and builds us up to the capacity of our calling. We need that time with Him to not burn out or become dependent on man for our identity. Seek and you will find Him, the truest form of Him, a loving Father.

Reflection:
Father, is there any way I am seeing You through eyes filtered by my life experience or the world's views?

CHAPTER 3

The Bread

Then Jesus declared, "I am the bread
of life. Whoever comes to me will
never go hungry, and whoever believes
in me will never be thirsty.

John 6:35 NIV

It is easy for us to come to Jesus, to talk to Jesus, and to welcome Him into the room. However, for much of the Body, doing the same with the Father can be thought of as terrifying or even blasphemous. So often we recognize the half-truths, inconsistencies, or uncertainties in what is taught to be acts of Christian faith. We are afraid to ask about them, often believing they are either the only one who sees it or that they are missing something everyone else knows. In reality, most of what we were taught probably started out as one man's preference and became doctrine. Take for example folding hands in prayer. It is nowhere to be found in the Bible. It is commonly thought to have originated some 800-plus years ago as a sign of humility when peasants begged for food. Instead, the Bible instructs us to lift holy hands in prayer. Thankfully, Jesus never requires us to beg; He simply says come to me. Often, we end up throwing ourselves down at His feet in reverence and thanksgiving, but not as a shame-filled disgrace who is hoping for the crumbs. I am not saying it is wrong to fold your hands in prayer, but instead pointing out one of many traditions that are held without biblical backing. Some have no problems, others seriously hinder the body of Christ from moving forward boldly.

The baker, who is the girl's best friend, is Jesus. He is the bread of life, He is the cornerstone and taught the girl many things. She lived near the bakery and stayed as close to the baker as she could at all times. She came to Him often and was always fed and satisfied. He listened to her fears and encouraged her to taste and see that the King is good (Encourage- en-to put in, courage-the ability to face your fears). He is the voice of truth in the midst of a well-meaning Kingdom. He drew her into love and showed her the way to no longer be an orphan. Jesus led her to the Father.

Jesus is the perfect example of the Father. He is love, joy, peace, patience, kindness, goodness, faithfulness, gentleness, and self control-as is the

Father. In a word, He is love. The Word reveals to us the love of the Father and the truth of His approachability in many ways. Let's look at a few.

Philip said, "Lord, show us the Father
and that will be enough for us.

Jesus answered: "Don't you know me, Philip, even after I have been among you such a long time? Anyone who has seen me has seen the Father. How can you say, 'Show us the Father'? Don't you believe that I am in the Father, and that the Father is in me? The words I say to you I do not speak on my own authority. Rather, it is the Father, living in me, who is doing his work. Believe me when I say that I am in the Father and the Father is in me; or at least believe on the evidence of the works themselves. Very truly I tell you, whoever believes in me will do the works I have been doing, and they will do even greater things than these, because I am going to the Father. And I will do whatever you ask in my name, so that the Father may be glorified in the Son.

John 14:8-13 NIV

The Son is the radiance of God's glory
and the exact representation of His
nature, upholding all things by His
powerful word. After He had provided

purification for sins, He sat down at the
right hand of the Majesty on high.

Hebrews 1:3 NIV

The son is the radiance of Father God's glory. Allow
that to settle in for a moment. Glory is the splendor,
holiness, and majesty of God. As you reflect on
the last chapter, chew on that for a moment. Jesus
is seen as warm, loving, and welcoming, but He
is the splendor, holiness, and the majesty of God!
God's majesty is the warmth, love, and comfort
of Jesus! Hebrews 1:3 says that Jesus is the exact
representation of God's nature. His good, kind
nature. Opposed to injustice but lovingly welcoming
the most down-and-out sinners, the castaways, the
prostitutes, and the demonized into His presence.
We cannot look at God as a stone-faced angry Father
and also look at Jesus as a compassionate and gentle
friend. He is as faithful, loving, and kind as Jesus. He
is good.

I am reminded of when I went to get my passport.
The instructions said to bring two copies of the
passport photo along with you, so I printed two
identical copies of the same photo. The clerk looked
at the top one and said it was an awful photo. She
then looked at the second and said, "This one is

better we will use it."

It was hard not to laugh at the absurdity; however, that is how many people view Jesus and the Father. They look at the Father and assume He can be terrible, hard, and angry. They look at His son, the exact representation of the Father, and see love, joy, and kindness.

Jesus takes us to the Father. He said, "No one can come to the Father except through me." Jesus is the bread of life which we can be sustained in. His nurturing and nourishment are what we need to be satisfied. As we fill ourselves on Jesus, we take in His being and become more like Him.

In holy communion, we take of His flesh and drink of His blood allowing what we eat to become a part of us. It is a physical act of a much deeper spiritual happening than we will ever know this side of eternity. Skeptics would ask if half an ounce of juice could change your body permanently. I would respond with, "What if it was a half ounce of poison?" There is so much power in taking communion that many people have found themselves healed of infirmities after taking communion. It is not just the taking of communion that Jesus desires. He desires us to commune with Him, dwelling in His presence, speaking and listening for Him to speak. His words are the very words of life. When we consume them and breathe them out we walk in communion with Jesus. He also desires that we walk in community with other believers, unselfishly, in holiness, and in remembrance of Him. These are all ways we have communion with Jesus daily.

> *"I am the living bread that came down from heaven. If anyone eats of this bread, he will live forever. And this bread, which I will give for the life of the world, is My flesh."*

John 6:51 ESV

Jesus gave of His very own flesh to be the bread of life to the world, that anyone who comes to Him may freely fill up on Him and have eternal life. Could it be that when Jesus was teaching how to pray, the daily bread He instructed us to ask for was more of Him? Allow Him to fill you by going to Him each day. In the story, the orphan girl went to the baker each day, in fact, she went several times a day. Each time she went He would give her more bread than she could carry, He would listen to her and give her advice. The more we go to Him and commune with Him the more we change from the inside out and become like Him.

Reflection:
Jesus, what have I been consuming instead of the bread of life?

CHAPTER 4

What's On The Table?

*When one of those who reclined at table with him
heard these things, he said to him, "Blessed is everyone
who will eat bread in the kingdom of God!"*
Luke 14:15 ESV

Food has a vast representation in the Kingdom. Food always represents good or bad. Good fruit, bad fruit. Enough food, too little food, or supernatural provision. Celebration, reliance, clean, and unclean. Repeatedly God instructed His people to celebrate with food. Eating with others was so important that it represented commitment, relationship, and acceptance. This is still a value held by many cultures though not as common in the Western world. Eating a meal together signified a relationship had been established and confirmed to the world.

You would be considered as unclean as a heathen if you ate with a sinner in Old Testament times, but Jesus came to destroy that mindset and ate with the immoral to show His love and openness to accepting them. He opened the feasts up to them.

In the Kingdom, a table is laid before us with an abundance of good food available to us. This feast is spiritual food and gifts. Everything is laid out before us as children of God to freely feast on. It never runs out and is always fresh. No matter how many children grab from the table, there is still plenty for everyone, you can never get full, and there is no such thing as greed. Fill up, because there is enough for everyone to take a fill larger than the most lavish Thanksgiving feast you have ever experienced!

God has shown me the table many times to reveal to me what is available to us as His loved children. He has revealed some of the food to be healing, peace, joy, prophecy, dreams, deliverance, and encounters among other things.

One of the first times I witnessed an in-depth deliverance that consisted of more than yelling in a person's face for the demon to flee, I began running through scriptures in my mind to make sure it lined up with the Word. I could only think through scriptures that aligned with what was taking place. However, to give me even more confidence at the moment, God showed the table spread before me and pointed to a place on the table where deliverance sat as part of the feast. He simply said, "it's available to you." I grabbed onto a piece of that dish and feasted on His goodness. If you have not been involved in a deliverance that may sound completely absurd-especially if your idea of deliverance is based on Hollywood's exorcist movies.

How can a deliverance taste of His goodness? I will tell you! When you see a person who has lived in torment for decades receive freedom, feel the release of pain and torment they have carried for decades, or even feel the love of the Father for the first time, you see His goodness. When you see a person whose chest was so restricted by the demonic take in a deep breath and feel the tension go, you see the affection of the Father. When they receive that freedom and weep under His presence, when you feel the presence of God fill the room in weighty glory as He restores what was damaged, you will taste and see His goodness in deliverance! I dare you to try it sometime, it's a wonderful dish. This is just one example of an endless supply of what is on the table.

Healing is another platter being served generously. My husband and I went on a journey to discover if healing was on the table many years ago. We began seeking out anyone who had claimed to see miraculous healings. We became familiar with Randy Clark, Heidi Baker, and others who hold a revelation of the healing love of the Father. We listened to their stories and how they moved in miracles, then we began to test it out. Pretty soon we saw miracles begin to happen. At first, it was seemingly small things like headaches and sore muscles that are huge to the person receiving healing. Then it moved to bigger things like seeing the mute speaking, the blind seeing, and documented health issues disappearing, confirmed by doctors. Each of these miracles resulted in the person knowing God as a Father who is near and who is concerned with their well-being. Often these stories would spread and hit an unbeliever square in the forehead with a decision to make: "Do I believe what I am seeing, my friend who had this permanent issue now healed? Or do I deny it because it doesn't fit in my box?" This is the reason and purpose for miracles. He desires to make His name known and to see His children whole and well.

I have heard people question the necessity of the miraculous stating that we have medical facilities and "advancements" that make them unnecessary. A touch from the Father is always necessary. It is as necessary as a child receiving affection from their parents!

When Jesus walked the earth prior to His resurrection He healed everyone who came to Him. He met their needs out of compassion and love.

> Great crowds came to him, bringing the
> lame, the blind, the crippled, the mute
> and many others, and laid them at his
> feet; and he healed them. The people

were amazed when they saw the mute
speaking, the crippled made well, the
lame walking and the blind seeing.
And they praised the God of Israel.

Matthew 15: 30-31 NIV

He chose to heal them even when it was inconvenient or would cause rebuke by the religious leaders, why? Because His love for the world is greater than we can fathom. His love that led Jesus to the cross to die for the salvation of those He loves. That love restores: relationally, physically, emotionally, and spiritually. And so, He sets a table for us to feast freely and share the good food with others.

In 2017, I had the pleasure of going to Kenya on a mission trip. In an area where Christianity is a mile wide but only an inch deep, they knew of Jesus but intermingled Him with other religions and practices. Upon meeting a young lady who was living in a compound run by a witch we learned that she could not speak aside from an unintelligible mumble because of an incident over a decade prior in which a curse was placed on her. We prayed over her and that night God revealed a word of knowledge about the curse. I declared those curses broken and saw her a few days later. That day as we were leaving she let out a clear but quiet "kwaheri," goodbye in Swahili. To our amazement, she was speaking though still a little mumbled and very quiet. We prayed for her again two more times. The last day I was in Kenya, she came for lunch along with dozens of others.

As I walked through the crowd greeting each person with my best "habari?" or, "Hello, how are you?" I stopped by her and said, "Hello, how are you?" in English. To my astonishment, she responded in English a loud clear, "I am well, how are you?" She was now speaking clearly and in two languages. I inquired as to how, she explained that she had been in school prior to the curse being placed on her, and she recalled the language.

This is one of many many stories I have had the joy of witnessing. God still restores. He loves His children and wants to see them free of curses and infirmities. He wants us to be Kingdom ambassadors spreading Heaven wherever we go and we do that by feasting on every good thing He lays before us.

Take a taste and see that He is good and supplies every good thing to those He loves.

Reflection:
Father, what is on the table that you would like me to try next?

CHAPTER 5

Stepping In, Stepping Away

Bless the LORD, O my soul, And forget
not all His benefits: Who forgives all your
iniquities, Who heals all your diseases,
Who redeems your life from destruction,
Who crowns you with lovingkindness
and tender mercies, Who satisfies your
mouth with good things, So that your
youth is renewed like the eagle's.

Psalms 103:2-5 NKJV

I hope you have begun to see the good things
the Father desires for us even now. At this point,
you are probably wondering why you do not see
more Christians sharing the feast or talking about
all the great benefits that are lavished upon us.
Unfortunately, as the Bible tells us, we will see
people come against us when we start to truly boldly
walk out the fullness of the gospel message. Many in
the church have been taught for so long that the only

benefit of Jesus is eternal life and happiness after death. Getting past this unbiblical mindset causes irritation as people begin to experience that there is more, and God is the God of now, the same God who said, "on earth as it is in Heaven," meant Heaven can manifest on Earth now.

Many people have come to believe that there is more to Christianity than just salvation at death and going to church once a week. They excitedly begin to explore it, only to be shut down, or worse, kicked out of their church community as it goes against the church's beliefs. Worse yet, when a believer gets shut down and told it is not of God, they have already seen the supernatural and desire more. This is where the New Age movement has gained most of its following. Those who are raised in dry religion that are then told the prophetic word they received or the healing they saw was not of God then turn to where they can be accepted and move in the giftings they were given. Only now, their gift is being used of and by evil.

Jesus himself said that there are those who would be persecuted for righteousness sake (being right in the sight of God) but the one who stands firm to the end will be saved. Later, He stated that if the world hates you, know that it hated Him first. Why did the world hate Jesus, the perfect image of God who is love itself? Because He irritated religious mindsets. He did things outside of tradition and was known for His miracles and simple teaching that made the Kingdom available to the simple people. They hated the simplicity and lack of apparent grandeur. They despised what appeared to be a simple man with no army or might. They could not see with spiritual eyes to see the King of Kings who took away the sin of the world. They wanted a messiah that would take over the earthly kingdoms with power and put them, the Jews, on a higher pedestal. They wanted to be Romans but with their God. They misinterpreted scripture to make it sound like what they wanted and not what God had foretold.

The very being of Jesus came against their dreams of what the true Messiah would be. He came as a humble man to give His life and the power He came in was that which brought healing, freedom, and a loving acceptance of those the religious crowd cast away. Often, we find the ones moving into the Kingdom now find the same backlash. It is often the ex-addict, the former witch, the less educated, but always the humble who come moving in the power of God and calling for Heaven on Earth. Just like in Jesus' time, this irritates the religious spirit.

After hearing far more stories than I can count of the transitions people have gone through as they began walking in Kingdom authority, I can tell you the common theme. While I hope and pray that it is not something you would have to walk through, there is a very real reality to the backlash of walking in the authority that you should be aware of.

People will notice something is different fairly rapidly as your prayer life changes, you are more confident in your identity, and the Bible comes to life for you.

People may question your motives and deny that the power of God is still at work today, they may argue that seeking the truth of scripture to be revealed is being overly religious or makes you a Jesus Freak (the song Stick to the Status Quo from High School Musical comes to mind). You will realize quickly that people are uncomfortable with what they don't yet understand and will spend their days trying to deny it, often loudly.

At this point, many people realize they are not welcome in the church they once called home, or worse, they are asked to leave. Friendships may become uncomfortable as some of your closest friends see the backlash and choose to stick with the "safety" of the status quo, and some will pull away completely. Like the Pharisees of Jesus day, many have created ideas of who Jesus is from their religious upbringing and not from scripture.

The good news is, there are many who have been in your shoes before and there is a very welcoming and loving community of believers who have chosen to not just live in the outskirts of the kingdom but to live fully alive in it, but that's not all! Forget not His benefits. The one who heals, the one who redeems, the one who forgives your iniquities, the one who fills your mouth with good things, and who crowns you with lovingkindness and mercy, He is with you to the end of the age - and He is so good!

He is the best friend, an encourager, and one who will smile alongside you as you see the sick healed, the demonized set free, the dead raised, and the gospel of the good news proclaimed. The good news of a loving God who sent His son to establish a never-ending government that is ever advancing and still active.

As you step into the castle, you will realize that you may find it feels like you are stepping away from those who came into the Kingdom but refused the castle. You will come to a balance and learn to have conversations that are sweet like honey and invite others into the intimacy you have learned. Pause and ask yourself how you would have responded to these conversations before you knew what you know now, before you saw the Kingdom at hand. This will help you to better relate to those you are speaking to and keep you from stepping away and leaving a worthwhile relationship.

Reflection:
Father, how can I share the reality of the Kingdom of Heaven at hand with words like honey?

CHERISH BICKEL

CHAPTER 6

Walking In Kingdom Identity

"As King's kids we have access to the
provisions of Heaven and from that
position, we choose to lay our lives
down. That's the humility that produces
lasting wisdom and gives birth to
a sustainable life of ministry."

Steve & Sally Wilson, Humility

I remember when I was at a time where I was coming into a better revelation of my identity I was asked to speak to a room full of former addicts. It was a crowded dining room packed with men, some of which had just been released from jail that morning, others awaiting trial for murder, and many just hoping to get their children back. They had all grown up in the Bible Belt. They knew felt-board Jesus and that He loves them, but they had no idea what God says about them. They know that He is a chain breaker, but not the application of those statements. The one piece that could change how they walk out the door, a knowledge of who they are in Christ was what they needed more than anything. Romans tells us that all of creation is groaning, waiting in eager expectation for the children of God to come into a full revelation of our identity. It is that important; it is an earth-shaking revelation!

I dropped the bomb on them that evening. I informed them that once they are saved their title is no longer "sinner" but instead a child of God. You could hear a pin drop. You could feel the tension and anger rise in a few as every religious bone in their body wanted to argue that they were in fact still a sinner, still an addict. I shared many scriptures allowing the Word to speak for itself, and the men began to breathe again. Once finished, I activated them in that identity, teaching them to listen for the voice of God and inviting Him to share a prophetic word with them. They were uncertain at first, but then began to release many prophetic words over each other and even several very accurate words to my husband and me. In fact, some of those words became the hope we needed to get through the next season of our lives. I am still in contact with many of those men and several have pointed to that moment as a defining moment in coming into a better knowledge of the reality of God! All they needed was a revelation of who they were created to be, children of God, not sinners.

Walking in true identity, and moving in the giftings given to us releases a greater knowledge of God to those who are around. When someone witnesses a healing or an accurate prophetic word, or better yet, gets healed or receives a prophetic word that they had been longing for, they realize that God does see them and cares for them. It is not just about us, but about the ones around us. As we release the Kingdom we see the Kingdom advance in ways that a sermon alone could not impact. In 1 Corinthians 2:4-5 Paul states,

...and my speech and my preaching was not with enticing words of man's wisdom, but in demonstration of the Spirit and of power: that your faith should not stand in the wisdom of men, but in the power of God.

Demonstrating the power of God is a part of sharing the gospel so that the wisdom of men is not the only part holding the knowledge. Seeing the power of God at work takes the gospel from wisdom and knowledge to an undeniable truth deep into the heart.

Walking in identity looks like something, but not everyone walking in identity will look the same. The common threads will be honor, humility, and a love of Christ that compels respect, service, and compassion for others. Many will see signs and wonders move in power when they minister to others, but all will know their identity as a child of

God. They know that He is a Father who loves His children listens to them and responds to them. He is one who desires good things for them, and they will know this unshakable truth to their core.

The dream I shared at the beginning of this book was a direct story from the Father to me one night. I woke up with such a deep groaning to know more, to understand more of the details, and to seek Him out all the more. Over time He has revealed more and more to me. He continues to add to that story in dreams and visions helping me to understand more about the Kingdom and what is available to us as believers. I held onto that dream as a deeply personal story until He told me it was time to release it. It has been something I have so treasured in my heart that releasing it has probably been one of my most vulnerable moments. He is ready, however, for His children to come to the revelation of what is available and begin to seek out for themselves what He has for them. He desires each one to come abide with Him so closely that they know His heartbeat.

One of the things He has revealed to me was access to all He has. Freedom to go about the castle and use whatever I need. There is no concern that I would use something incorrectly, lose it, or break it. Remember, there is no lack in the Kingdom, there is plenty to go around, therefore, no fear of overusing gifts when done with a pure heart.

When someone comes to my home to do service work, they do not get to walk into my kitchen and grab a snack without me first offering it. They don't have the freedom to grab a coat from my bedroom close,t and they certainly can not climb in my lap and take a midday rest. A servant doesn't have these freedoms, but a child? My children can come and go freely from room to room and eat as they need, they use all I have for their comfort and climb into my lap when they need a hug or to rest in the safety of a loving parent's arms. Oftentimes, they will even use what I have to help others. I would say most of my closest friends have the same privileges whether they realize it or not.

If you grew up in a strict home or a home where perfection was expected this may be a hard reality to process. Some may have even heard the reprimand, "Be perfect, therefore, as your heavenly Father is perfect." In this passage, Jesus is telling His disciples to love their enemies and to respond with prayer for those who persecute them, an act of maturity. The word perfect is "teleios" which means finished, complete, or mature. He doesn't expect perfection as the world sees it but does ask for a growing maturity of our love for others. In that maturity, we know how to use the gifts for love and are even willing to pray for healing for the one who may be persecuting us.

Even in immaturity, for those growing into the maturity and fullness in Christ, there is grace for when we mess up. I am sure we have all had a heart check after walking away from a situation and knowing we had an opportunity to pray and didn't. It's an opportunity to grow further in your maturity. Once we realize that place we are lacking love or compassion, we can see the opportunity to grow (and if you never notice an area to grow you might want to ask a good friend if you are prideful or arrogant-another opportunity for growth).

You won't ever go wrong revealing the love of the Father to others. Signs, wonders, and miracles are ways He allows us to bring Heaven to earth demonstrating His love in power. They are signs that identify those who follow Him just as much as our love for one another makes known to the world who we are, heirs of God and co-heirs with Christ. To walk in this identity will be apparent in our confidence, peace, joy, and love, as well as how we display the Kingdom of God that is at hand, here and now.

Reflection: Father, how do You see me in the Kingdom? Where do You want me to be?

CHERISH BICKEL

CHAPTER 7

From Riches to Rags

You have received a spirit of adoption,
through which we cry, "Abba Father!" The
Spirit itself bears witness with our spirit
that we are children of God, and if children,
then heirs, heirs of God and joint-heirs
with Christ, if only we suffer with him so
that we may also be glorified with him.

Romans 8:15-17 ESV

If you speak to someone who has adopted a
child, you will find that it is rarely a smooth
process. Unfortunately, the orphan spirit roots deep
into the psyche causing children to revert back
to previous behaviors or self-protective reactions.
Often children who were in nutritionally deficient
environments will hoard food years after being in
a healthy home. One moment of stress can trigger
the behavior to start again. Many of us have seen
another form of this in grandparents who lived

through the Great Depression. Hoarding became a huge problem decades later as the children of that era became adults that had a fear of going without.

When we step into Kingdom living, we are so excited at first to have a healthy family and a loving Father. One day, something comes along and sidetracks us. Before we know it we are thinking in orphan terms. Feelings of being less than others or unworthy of the things God is pouring out, or even confusion about where we belong begin to mount up. Most of us will find ourselves at some point having put the orphan clothing back on. Retreating to what we had always known, hiding in the shadows and thinking we are only good enough for the crumbs off the floor, and being pleased to take what we can get. We walk around the castle knowing the goodness of God but feeling like we are not worthy of belonging. We then put on a coat of shame trying to hide how we really feel but in reality, just add another layer of orphan clothes to the mix.

In case no one has told you, you belong. You are welcome in the house. You are free to eat and be satisfied, free to dance down the hallways, free to climb up in the Father's lap and tell Him about your day. Welcome home, we have been waiting for you!

Notice that in the dream a fellow child pointed out the orphan mentality. Sometimes Holy Spirit will show us, and other times it may be a brother or sister in Christ gently asking you why you seem down, often they see right through it. Rejection, abandonment, jealousy, feeling like everyone is growing more than you, feeling like you are not worthy of His love and gifts or like you have to prove yourself, feeling like everyone else receives more than you (more revelation, recognition, power, etc.) these are a few of the more common signs you may have an orphan mindset or wounds that need to be healed to stand confidently in your true identity.

When you recognize these areas affecting your identity, speak to a mentor or someone firmly settled in their identity and allow them to pray with you and walk you into the process of healing the wounds that caused that way of thinking. Some of it is rooted in poor theology and other areas you will find resulted from childhood wounds or church hurt. Many people find incredible shifts in their thinking after going through a deliverance as the demonic's primary goal is to make you forget who you are.

Present the thoughts you struggle with to God and ask for His truth, then wait and listen for His answer. One of my favorite prayers to pray is, "search me, oh God, and find if there is any offensive way in me." Then I wait and allow Him to reveal areas I have wrong thinking.

His Spirit bears witness that we are His children, any other voice or thought that is contrary to His witness is false. He may reveal an area of sin or woundedness, but it will be done in love and conviction, not in condemnation and shame.

> "We demolish arguments and
> every pretension that sets itself up
> against the knowledge of God, and
> we take captive every thought to
> make it obedient to Christ."

2 Corinthians 10:5 NIV

Knowing who we are in Christ is part of the knowledge of God and who He is, His character. He desires not that we would just know *of* God but that we would *know* God, and this is where our true identity is built. As we grow to know God and realize who He is, we become more like Him and discover our true identity. He longed to walk among the Garden with Adam and Eve, and He continually reiterated that desire throughout the Old Testament. What joy it must have been when Jesus was born of flesh, and God could walk among man again as He desired.

> "*The Lord bless* (kneel down before) *you*
> *and keep* (guard, to hedge about with thorns) *you;*
> *the Lord make his face* (entire being, countenance)
> *shine* (divide light from darkness) *on you*

and be gracious (show favor) *to you;*
the Lord lift (to lift continually, to carry) *his*
face (entire being, countenance) *toward you*
and give (cause to be established) *you*
peace (complete wholeness)."

This is the blessing that was given to Aaron and his sons to recite over the Israelites in Numbers 26. It was the job of the priests to pronounce this blessing daily over the people and is still pronounced daily in Jewish synagogues. So much of the depth of the original Hebrew gets lost in translation that many scholars spend their lives trying to reveal more accurate translations of each word.

God's goal all along was for His children to mature into looking more like Him simply by allowing His countenance to shine upon them. When we come face to face with the King, light and dark are divided, we begin to see how He has guarded us, we see the favor of God upon our lives, our face begins to carry His countenance, and wholeness becomes manifest in our life.

We cannot walk face to face with God, listen to His truth about our lives, and still see ourselves as orphans. Allow His truth to flood your heart today. Allow Him to reveal His closeness and the revelation of who you were created to be to wash over you.

Reflection:
Father, is there any area in which I am putting the orphan clothes back on or never changed them, to begin with?

CHAPTER 8

Taking Your Place at the Table

The Lord is my shepherd;
I have all that I need.
He lets me rest in green meadows;
he leads me beside peaceful streams.
He renews my strength.
He guides me along right paths,
bringing honor to his name.
Even when I walk
through the darkest valley,
I will not be afraid,
for you are close beside me.
Your rod and your staff
protect and comfort me.
You prepare a feast for me
in the presence of my enemies.
You honor me by anointing my head with oil.
My cup overflows with blessings.
Surely your goodness and unfailing love will pursue me
all the days of my life,
and I will live in the house of the Lord
Forever.

Psalm 23 NLT

Reread Psalm 23, slowly this time. David understood something that very few understood in his time. He was a man after God's own heart before it was popular. His writings were both born out of his affection towards God and prophetic in nature, poured out of David's relationship with Him. God was calling out a man into a deeper relationship and revelation of His love. He desired us long before we knew of Him. This was shown again in Song of Solomon as a declaration of love and pursuit is sung out.

First, we are assured we have all we need. No more striving, no beating the plow to survive. We are supplied with all our needs, and we can rest. God doesn't just allow us to rest, He calls us into it and tells us to be still and know that He is God, to rest in Him. He calls us into physical and spiritual rest. He sets aside a day every week for us to physically rest and tells us that we are to cease striving and know that He is God. He has everything taken care of.

Then we are assured that no matter the valley we walk through, He is with us, guiding, comforting, and leading. Not only that, even in dark places, God prepares a table, a feast in front of the enemies. A dichotomy of visuals. When we are in the presence of enemies, we have every guard up, we are ready for battle. But He places a table and tells us to set down our sword and shield to eat.

When I read this, I see a front line battle. Two opposing armies face each other preparing to attack. Then the King of Kings walks out and sets up a huge wooden table - a ridiculously ornate table for the battlefield scene. It is made of a thick solid piece of wood with carvings and broad legs. It had to have taken an entire army just to carry it out to the field. You cannot fit a feast on a small table, after all.

He puts a feast greater than any Christmas feast out before His child and pulls up a chair. I sit and feast on good food as the enemy camp watches, drooling and hungry, their slop for dinner hardly holding them over. It is a slap in the face to the adversary. Not only do they know they are going to be defeated, they watch the victorious ones feasting in the presence of the King. To further the insult, He anoints His children with oil, a sign and marking of honor and kingship, a silent but blatant declaration that His children rule over all of the enemy camp, and they will stand victoriously. It is beautiful.

Unfortunately, false humility has overtaken much of the
church. In the name of humility, we place ourselves as unworthy of such things, disregarding that Christ died to make us worthy. Overlooking that the Spirit of the living God resides in us. It hinders us from receiving the next few verses of Psalm 23;

My cup overflows with blessings. Surely your goodness

*and unfailing love will pursue me all the days of my
life, and I will live in the house of the Lord forever.*

This isn't a prosperity gospel, but it is a promise that
God will supply all of our needs. It is repeated by the
apostle Paul in Philippians 4:19:

*And my God will supply every need of yours
according to his riches in glory in Christ Jesus,"*

and again in 2 Corinthians 9:8:

*...and God is able to bless you abundantly, so
that in all things at all times, having all that you
need, you will abound in every good work.*

He not only supplies our needs but goodness
(pleasant, valuable, prosperity, & happiness),
unfailing love (mercy, kindness, lovingkindness,
and favor), and blessings (wealth) will pursue us
all the days of our lives. A Father who wants good
things for His children, one who will supply all their
needs, and often give them their heart's desires is
wanting you to be open to His blessings.

Not only is it pushed that we should not be blessed
in a financial manner, but also that the love the
Father lavishes on us should not be tangible. For
many people who have experienced this kind of
love from the Father, they feel unable to share the
experience with others. However, as we share our
experiences it invites others into that kind of deep

intimacy with the Lord.

When we begin taking our place at the table, we stop seeing the constant battle before us and shift our focus to the host, Yahweh Sabaoth, the Lord of Hosts/Armies who goes before us. Our focus on Him shifts our entire being, no longer worn from battle we find rest in Him and can fight from that place at the table, feasting, laughing, and filled with joy in the presence of the King of Kings, our victorious one.

> "For the LORD your God is he that goes with you, to fight for you against your enemies, to give you the victory."

Deuteronomy 20:4 ESV

Rest in Him and boldly take your place at the table set before you and feast on His goodness in the presence of your enemies. No more striving, fear, and weariness. He has a place set just for you.

Reflection:
Father, show me how I can rest in you even on the

battlefield.

CHAPTER 9

The Place of Honor

Do nothing out of selfish ambition or vain
conceit, but in humility consider others
better than yourselves. Each of you should
look not only to your own interests, but
also to the interests of others. Your attitude
should be the same as that of Christ Jesus:
Who, being in very nature God, did not
consider equality with God something to be
grasped, but made himself nothing, taking
the very nature of a servant, being made
in human likeness. And being found in
appearance as a man, he humbled himself
and became obedient to death-even death
on a cross! Therefore God exalted him to
the highest place and gave him the name
that is above every name, that at the name
of Jesus every knee should bow, in heaven
and on earth and under the earth, and
every tongue confess that Jesus Christ
is Lord, to the glory of God the Father.

Philippians 2:3-11 ESV

Honor is so important in the Kingdom that some would even say that honor is the currency of Heaven. Our Western view has a very different idea of honor than the Eastern view and it is even further from the community standards of honor that were expected in the time of Jesus and prior. Honor at that time was a value of the family unit and community, not just an individual. If a person did something sinful, it was a disgrace to the whole community, a falling out of the grace of other communities.

Often, millennials and younger have a very limited idea of what honor is and place it along the same lines as respect. True honor not only respects an individual through admiring qualities and achievements, but also views others as more significant than one's own self. Honor sees what God has placed in others and calls that out. Honor lets others sit in the highest seat, and receive recognition and applause from the heart not out of a feeling of insignificance. Honor sees that others are made great by the graces of God, just as they have been made great, and seeks to raise others not just to where they are, but even higher. This is also a sign of a great leader.

"When you are invited to a wedding banquet, do not sit in the place of honor, in case someone more

distinguished than you has been invited."
Luke 14:8 NIV

Jesus was saying, don't assume you are the best of the best. Place others in higher regard than yourself and look to show honor to others above yourself. If you get a chance to step back and shine a light on others' achievements, do it! Be humble and continually go lower.

We are told to honor our father, mother, widows, all people, the King, the Son, and the Father. Honor is to see the true value of someone, a value they may not even see in themselves. In the Kingdom, we no longer see others as the world sees them, but rather we see through the lens of Holy Spirit, and we see the value God has placed on them. A value so high that He sent His only son to die for them. He paid the highest price so the lowliest of sinners could sit by Him in the heavenlies!

Honor all people.
Love the brotherhood.
Fear God.
Honor the king.

1 Peter 2:17 KJV

In his book, *Culture of Honor*, Danny Silk shifts the paradigm of authority by adding in true honor.

Traditional authority places a person over another and the lower person must honor and respect the one above them. Honor, while still leaving room for authority, places not only the value of where the other is at now, but also adds the value of who they are called to be. "In a culture of honor, leaders lead with honor by courageously treating people according to the names God gives them and not according to the aliases they receive from people." (*Culture of Honor*, by Danny Silk)

It calls us out of our past and into our future. A culture of honor allows for mistakes and sees it as an opportunity for growth and maturity. Culture says, "Make a mistake and you will pay for it." Honor says, "You made a mistake? Let's fix this together and learn from it."

Romans 12:10 says to outdo each other in showing honor. This isn't talking about talking each other up, it is not slimy promotion; it is a genuine building up of one another because you see the great value and call on each other's lives. You look at another person and see them as a son or daughter of God and are in awe of what He is doing in and through them. When you see that in others and allow His heart for them to fill yours, honor will flow naturally. You will begin to encourage them not with false flattery but out of deep respect for what you see Christ doing in and through them. The prophetic adds to this so beautifully when you ask the Father His heart for His children and He reveals a piece of that to you; you cannot help but view the individual in a different light, the light of Heaven. This type of honor also opens up the doors of access to a person's life.

How do we honor in a community or culture that does not show mutual honor? The same way we do in a culture of honor. Ask God to reveal His value for an individual and love them as the Father loves them. Bestow Heavenly honor upon them and allow God to reveal to the hearts of man what He has planned. Choose to honor even the ones who belittle. Only speak about the positive traits of a person and do not gossip. Raise them up by holding yourself to a higher standard.

In his book, *A Tale of Three Kings*, Gene Edwards outlines the honor David showed Saul. Despite having been anointed to be king, David never fought *for* kingship, he dared not even attack the one who had come to kill him when he had the chance. He chose to honor and waited on the Lord to reveal his kingship at the proper time. He never attempted a revolt telling others to follow him in a better way, he honored the leadership which God currently had in place.

> "Who, then, can know who is a David and
> who is a Saul? God knows. But he won't tell.
> Are you so certain your king is a Saul and

not a David that you are willing to take the position of God and go to war against your Saul? If so, then thank God you did not live in the days of crucifixion. What, then, can you do? Very little. Perhaps nothing. However, the passing of time (and the behavior of your leader while that time passes) reveals a great deal about your leader. And the passing of time, and the way you react to that leader—be he David or Saul—reveals a great deal about you."

A Tale of Three Kings, by Gene Edwards

Honor reveals more about your character than the ones you honor. When faced with honor, a heart's true condition is revealed. Pride, arrogance, and conceit all start to rear their heads if they are around when placed with the option to honor another above yourself. We see this in Luke 22. The disciples had not only just finished the Passover meal with Jesus, they had just witnessed the Last Supper and declared that the Kingdom of God was imminent. Pride rose up and they began to argue over who is worthy to receive the most honor. We find this account in Luke 22:24-27:

A dispute also arose among them as to which of them was considered to be greatest. Jesus said to them, "The kings of the Gentiles lord it over them; and those who exercise authority over them call themselves Benefactors. But you are not to be like that. Instead, the greatest among you should be like the youngest, and the one who rules like the one who serves. For who is greater, the one who is at the table or the one who serves? Is it not the one who is at the table? But I am among you as one who serves."

Jesus clears the air, "I am among you as one who serves." He had just washed their feet, yet they still hadn't grasped the honor that serving bestows. Jesus, the King of Kings, the Messiah had stooped low to wash the feet of men who argue over being better than each other. Furthermore, He went to the cross and gave His life for them - the prostitutes, the addicts, the murderers, the pedophiles, and the religious. Always choose humility for self, and honor for others. Above all else, honor God.

Reflection:
Father, who can I honor better? How do You view them?

CHAPTER 10

Even Unto Death

Love bears all things, believes all things,
hopes all things, endures all things.

1 Corinthians 13:7 ESV

If honor is the currency of Heaven, then loyalty would be the merchandise. As honor is exchanged, loyalty builds, and they both flow from a heart set on the ways of God. Loyalty is one of the hardest disciplines to bear and often requires the empowering of Holy Spirit to walk us through trials and keep our hearts in a posture of love and connection. As those around us react out of pain and hurt or even out of ignorance, loyalty will set us apart. To love those who have lost every reason to be loved, to serve those who are not leading from a heart of service, and to show them honor is to be loyal.

There are times when you will be called away

from a toxic environment. We see this example with David. He didn't stay when Saul attempted to take his life by hurling spears at his head. He left, but he remained loyal to the king in that he did not revolt against him. We do not see him attempting to build an army to join his cause or leave with any of Saul's people. He did not strike Saul down when he had the chance, even when Saul had done everything to justify the attack and others were encouraging him to do so. David dared not harm God's anointed one.

> But David said to Abishai, "Don't destroy him! Who can lay a hand on the Lord's anointed and be guiltless? As surely as the Lord lives," he said, "the Lord himself will strike him, or his time will come and he will die, or he will go into battle and perish. But the Lord forbid that I should lay a hand on the Lord's anointed. Now get the spear and water jug that are near his head, and let's go."

1 Samuel 26:9-11 NIV

In the same way, we are called to show loyalty to others even when they hurt us. Every believer, after all, is a royal priest, chosen and set apart. As trials arise, it will often reveal pride in us that we need to lay down at the feet of Jesus, not only pride, but bitterness. As we begin to look for a way out of a relationship, we begin to recognize the things we held at high value, and often it was not honor but rather self. When we catch ourselves justifying talking bad about a person, it points to a root of pride that says, "I am better than them, they wronged me. I have a right to be angry, hurt, and to point out their faults to others." Pride will puff you up and make you feel like the victim or the good guy in the situation. Humility and honor will bring you low to serve the one who betrays.

Think about how David could have spun this story! I could hear him building an army by whispering to individuals, "I was anointed to be king. I am the rightful King, God said so. Saul has gone crazy, I think he is demonized! I went to serenade him, and he hurled a spear at me. He is jealous of me, out to kill me and anyone in his path to get to me." Look at that again, none of that is false information, but it also is not shared from a loyal and honoring heart. David was after the heart of God, not a throne, title, or position, and he chose to not speak against God's chosen one.

Are we seeking a throne, title, or position in our relationships? Or are we seeking the heart of God for the relationship? A relationship focused on what you receive from it will always end in destruction. However, a relationship firmly seated in honoring and serving the other will not only call them higher, but it will bring you along with it as well.

I want to take a moment to discuss unhealthy relationships. Always seek wise and godly counsel before making any decisions. There are times when you may need to get away from hurled spears. There are truly dangerous relationships that you may find yourself in. It is still possible to honor a person and remain loyal while cutting them off. For the longest time, I struggled with Exodus 12:20, "Honor your father and mother."

For the safety of my children, I had to walk away from these relationships. One day I was processing how hard that scripture is to hear because I felt dishonorable to my parents, but my priority is the safety of my children. A wise friend stated that I do honor them in the way I speak about them, by holding my head high, by not engaging in further destruction when they are being loud and public about issues, and by choosing forgiveness over and over again. It is possible to hold a place of honor, loyalty, and love for someone who you cannot remain in a relationship with. It is imperative to have a mentor, pastor, or counselor walk with you through this. Someone to help you process forgiveness; someone to watch and help keep your heart on track with love and not falling into the trap of bitterness.

Loyalty should be foundational to all relationships as it goes hand in hand with honor. The Bible tells us that there are friends that stick closer than a brother(Proverbs 18:24), that a friend loves at all times(Proverbs 17:17), and that greater love has none than this: to lay one's life down for their friend (John 15:13). Loyalty is standing beside someone even when they have done wrong and helping them work through the mess. Loyalty is not ignoring the mess or helping them live in denial of wrongdoings.

One of the many examples of loyalty we have in the Bible is in Ruth 1:16-17. Ruth tells Naomi, *"For where you go I will go, and where you lodge I will lodge. Your people shall be my people, and your God my God."* This is the depth of loyalty that God calls us to within covenant relationships. To serve God together and run through all that life throws at us. In serving Naomi loyally, Ruth finds a husband, the one who becomes the family redeemer. A husband was not promised if she stayed with Naomi; in fact, Ruth stood a better chance if she went back to her family's village, but still, she chose loyalty.

God is looking for loyal children who will be loyal in their relationships with others, and even more so, with Him. He wants laid-out lovers of Him who will proclaim His name even when it is bad for business, makes followers drop like flies, and even when it risks their life. He longs for loyalty that runs so deep we are not even swayed by the lusts of the world and are never dragged into the temptations of fitting in. We are holy, chosen, set apart, a new creation not of this world. Instead we carry the mind of Christ and a heart of flesh with His law on our hearts and minds and His Spirit dwelling in us. He desires us to love loyally as He loves, and He empowers us to do that with His spirit. With this, we can lay down our life surrendering all we can for the sake of His glory, loyally loving Him even unto death.

Reflection:
Father, who have you called me to walk in loyalty towards?

CHAPTER 11

The God Who Delights

The Lord your God is with you,
the Mighty Warrior who saves.
He will take great delight in you;
in his love he will no longer rebuke you,
but will rejoice over you with singing."
Zephaniah 3:17 NIV

As all of the prophets foretold, the old covenant relationship with God was changing. God desired a relationship with all people from the beginning, through human choices and fear, an authoritative covenant was made. Not one based on relationships but on rules and consequences. The Father's heart grieved. He longed for people who loved Him as He loved them. David saw it, the prophets spoke of it, then Jesus came to fulfill it. He connected humanity to the divine. He restored the relationship, removed the rebuke, then welcomed all to join in.

We have a glorious Father who delights over His children and declares it over them with singing - a ringing cry, a proclamation of joy. He sets a table before them with a feast available to all who want to join. A feast of every good and perfect gift from above.

He welcomes us into a Kingdom that is at hand, here and now, and its riches are available to us. His goodness and mercy are freely available, without limit. Jesus brought with Him an open Heaven, a torn veil where we have access to signs and wonders to reveal the Father to unbelievers and bring restoration to the believer. He lavished great love upon us, and He continues to daily.

He invites us into close communion with Him. We have access to the King of Kings every moment of every day - open communication. He empowers us to go forth, advancing the Kingdom of Heaven, seeing it manifest at the sound of a word spoken from authority granted straight from the throne room of Heaven. Seated in a place of authority, He lights our path and proclaims our destiny, calling out not what man sees, but what the Creator of Heaven and Earth knows.

"How great is the love the Father has lavished on us, that we should be called children of God! And that is what we are! The reason the world does not know us is that it did not know him."

1 John 3:1 NIV

The Father lavishes His love on us - more abundantly and beautifully than we can hope or imagine. He grants us our heart's desires and holds no good thing back from His children. He knows what is beneficial and needed, and He supplies every need.

His love fills believers with a peace that passes all understanding, a joy that flows even in times of trouble, and authority to walk in His ways. He knows our every anxious thought and quiets us with His love, singing over us a song of deliverance. He longs to gather His children under His wings, a shelter, a place of safety and strength.

All of this, and yet, He delights in us.

The Lord takes pleasure in those who fear Him, in those who hope in His steadfast love.
Psalm 147:11 ESV

He delights in His children and desires them to live in close communion with Him. So much so that He sent His one and only son that whoever believes in Him shall have everlasting life(John

3:16), living with the Father. But the promises of the New Covenant begin the moment we step foot into the Kingdom. The moment we accept His salvation and transfer our citizenship from the kingdom of darkness to light, those promises come over our life. However, we also have to make the choice to step into those promises, to walk in the giftings He has for His children.

The primary focus is and always will be relationships. Signs, wonders, and miracles should flow from that, but they are not the focus. Knowing the triune God in mind, heart, and communion is the most important part of your walk with Christ. It is not about how many people you evangelized, how many got healed, or how many demons you cast out. These things flow from the love of God, but they are not the focus. Were you in His presence today? Did you seek Him with all your heart? Did you allow Him to shape your thoughts, words, and actions to look more like Him today?

He is not just close. He is intertwined in our very being. Holy Spirit is within us breathing out the breath of Heaven as we breathe. He longs to hear your voice calling to Him and for you to listen for His response. He is Jehovah Shammah, the God who hears; El Roi, the God who sees you; Immanuel, God with us. He desires that we not just live in the Kingdom, but instead, in the castle, recognizing His closeness and abiding in communion with our

Father.

Reflection:

Father, what promises am I not currently walking in?

Where have I missed access to Heaven on Earth by not recognizing Your closeness?

My prayer for you is that these words will sink deep into your spirit and you will begin to see His very being near you in every part of every day. That you will begin to interact with Heaven on Earth so that Earth becomes like Heaven. I bless you to know the Father intimately and deeply. To trust Him with your whole life and let go of any unbilical mindsets or teachings.

- Cherish

MY DEEPEST APPRECIATION TO...

My husband and best friend, Robert, who encouraged (and pushed) me to write what was on my heart and mind. The one who walked side by side with me on this journey of this discovery. Thank you for being my personal cheerleader and biggest fan.

To my friend, Tiffany Fitzpatrick, for being the first one to tell me (repeatedly) that I was not only going to write a book, but that what needed to be written was already within me.

A special thanks and recognition to The Well family who lovingly creates a space for people to come explore and find their identity as sons and daughters. You welcomed us in and called us family.

Most importantly, my greatest treasure, my Heavenly Father. Thank you for loving me even when I was lost and afraid of You. In all my misunderstanding, You cared all the more.

ABOUT THE AUTHOR

Cherish Bickel

Cherish is first and foremost a daughter of the King. She loves to laugh, explore the beauty of God's creation, sing what she is doing, dance in the grocery store to 90's hits, bake brownies, beat everyone at board games and have long talks over coffee. Her greatest joy is sharing the powerful love of Christ, beginning with her family.

She is married to the guy she met at a coffee shop-as if in a Hallmark movie, and together they have 5 amazing children plus a wonderful son-in-law. Together, they have a passion to see the love of the Father cover the earth as the waters cover the seas. They long to go into all the world sharing His greatness with all creation.

www.ingramcontent.com/pod-product-compliance
Lightning Source LLC
Chambersburg PA
CBHW072009060426
42446CB00042B/2281